God Bless
Grandparents

The Adventures
of Being
a Grandparent

God Bless
Grandparents

Catharine Brandt

AUGSBURG Publishing House • Minneapolis

GOD BLESS GRANDPARENTS

Copyright ©1978 Augsburg Publishing House

Library of Congress Catalog Card No. 78-52189

International Standard Book No. 0-8066-1658-X

Scripture quotations unless otherwise noted are from the Revised Standard Version of the Bible, copyright 1946, 1952, and 1971 by the Division of Christian Education of the National Council of Churches. Quotations from the Living Bible (LB) copyright © 1971 by Tyndale House Publishers. Quotations from Today's English Version (TEV) copyright 1966 by American Bible Society. KJV means King James Version.

Permission to include quotations from the following books has been granted by the publishers:

Treat Me Cool, Lord by Carl F. Burke, © Association Press.

Lift Up Your Hearts by Herbert F. Brokering, © The Liturgical Press.

Photos: Wallowitch, pages 8, 68, 76; Camerique, 12, 120; Paul S. Conklin, 18; Jean-Claude Lejeune, 22; Daniel D. Miller, 30; Bob Combs, 38; Florence Sharp, 44; Paul M. Schrock, 48, 84; Toge Fujihira, 54; Harold M. Lambert, 58; H. Armstrong Roberts, 94, 108; Rohn Engh, 102.

MANUFACTURED IN THE UNITED STATES OF AMERICA

To my grandchildren
Cindy, Pam, Rose, Judy, Doug
and
Dan, Beth, Sharon, Bonnie, Gary

God Bless Grandparents

page   9   Preface

11   All-Star Grandparents

17   Reach for the Hearing Aids

25   Small Boats and Big Seas

31   Apprentice Grandparents

37   Creepers, Leapers, and Knee-Sitters

46   Looking for God's Autograph

51   Never a Dull Moment

61   A Bar of Yellow Soap

66   Put-Downs and Buildups

75   Cheering Section

84   "It Matches Me!"

91   Long-Distance Grandparents

99   Adventures on Wheels and at Home

106   Talking to God

111   After That the Dark?

118   Legacy

Preface

Being a grandparent is a breathtaking experience. Bringing surprises and shocks, laughter and tears, grandchildren also educate us. They dangle before us the beauty and wonder of childhood. They enlighten us, sharpen our wits, and open our eyes to the world as it is today.

Grandchildren provide us with some of our proudest occasions, some of our tenderest experiences, and, without question, some of our funniest moments.

One of the surest ways for grandparents to make the all-star lineup is to enjoy and support each grandchild, counting time spent together a privilege.

Wise grandparents are careful, though, not to build a life around their grandchildren. They keep hands off, showing love and enthusiasm, and growing along with their grandchildren.

The longer we grandparents live, the clearer we see

the hand of God in life. He instructs us in his Word to pass this vision on to our children's children. "One generation shall praise thy works to another, and declare thy mighty acts" (Ps. 145:4 KJV).

Not our own accomplishments, not stories of our travels or the great people we have known, not even wealth—we are to pass on awareness of the faithfulness and power of God.

My grandchildren still have growing and living ahead, and so have I. This book is a record, not only of my relationship with them, but also of stories of scores of grandparents I have talked to. It shows some of the tough spots grandparents work through and underscores right paths they have taken.

All-Star
Grandparents

From the moment the phone jangles and the message comes over the wire, life takes on a rainbow hue. "It's a girl!" or "It's a boy!" Or even what one young man said when he called his father long distance: "When you ask the Lord for something, he's apt to give more than you expect. Twins!"

As instant grandparents, most of us rush in with gifts, offers of help, and advice, all wrapped in love. We are determined to be award-winners.

Some of us never imagined how great the fringe benefits would be. Nor how much fun, in spite of shocks and tears along the way, nor what a learning experience being grandparents is. Grandchildren help us see ourselves in perspective—no easy feat when we wear trifocals and are inclined to watch the rearview mirror.

Carlyle reminds us, "From the days of the first grand-

father, everybody has remembered a golden age behind him!" The golden age for grandchildren is *now*, and if grandparents want to excel they have to merge into the present and grow a little themselves.

Nowadays there's no such thing as a typical grandparent. If we see somebody who looks like a grandfather, limping with a cane or sitting in the sun, he's probably a great-grandfather. More than the horse is outdated in the lines:

> To grandfather's house we'll go;
> The horse knows the way
> To carry the sleigh
> Through the white and drifted snow.

Today's grandparents are probably both working, or one lives alone in an apartment. They entertain grandchildren at McDonald's or with Kentucky Fried. Or grandparents are guests in their children's home. Stylishly dressed, they arrive in a compact car, with a spring in their step and grandmother fresh from the beauty shop. They bring presents that make them popular with grandchildren, and they leave before pandemonium and discipline take over.

Some grandparents have unusual occupations that endear them to grandchildren. Recently the papers carried a report of a fascinating grandmother who retired from her job as a long-distance truck driver. With two million miles of accident-free driving in her log, she won a citation from the American Trucking

Association. She retired, she said, "because I want to spend more time with my grandchildren."

Others are busy traveling, or just being themselves.

On a visit to her daughter's family, half a continent away, Ruth deplaned bearing gifts, hugs, kisses, and admiration for her grandchildren. One morning first-grader Kelley said, "Grandma, will you walk over to my school at recess so the kids can see my gorgeous grandma?"

Nothing loath, Ruth agreed. When the time came it was windy outside, so she tied a scarf around her head and borrowed an old jacket from her daughter. A dozen children pressed against the school yard fence.

"There she is," Kelley said. Ruth waved and talked to the children, who burst into a fit of giggling.

After school Kelley walked slowly into the house. "What's wrong?" her grandmother asked.

"The kids said you're not gorgeous." Then she flung herself into her grandmother's arms. "But I said you are too!" And that was all that mattered to Kelley and her grandmother.

All-star grandparents do have a few traits in common. Their hearts overflow with love for their grandchildren. They accept the children right where they are, not where they may be someday in the future.

Top-level grandparents are generous with admiration and praise. They refuse to carry disparaging information from one family to another. Achievements, yes. Failures, never. They stay up-to-date with what's going on in the world. And they keep hands off.

When I began to build a new life after my husband died, God showed me the healing process could be helped by the love of others, especially that of my grandchildren. When children are little, parents often need our help, and I was glad to oblige. I was, though, blissfully unaware of the pitfalls that lay ahead until a friend pointed them out to me.

"The trouble with being a grandparent," she said, "is that we are experienced but unemployed parents, and some of us would like to return to the job market." She added with a chuckle, "Part-time. The danger is that we depend on grandchildren to fulfill our need to be useful."

I took her words to heart. Already I knew my daughter and daughter-in-law had an easy aptitude with their babies that I had lacked as a young mother. They didn't need my help as much as I liked to think. Both sets of parents amazed me with their wisdom and resourcefulness. Watching them in action, I learned to keep my nose out of their lives.

Now I try to emulate a friend who has two grandchildren married and one in college. She says, "I work hard at being a person in my own right. I want my grandchildren to love me, not as a duty, but because we enjoy each other as friends."

New grandparents and old pros can resist building a life around their grandchildren. A woman with seven says, "I no longer depend on them to make me feel worthwhile. Instead I need them to help me break with the past as I try to understand their outlook on life."

As parents our aim was to help our children to independence. We cut the ties that bound them to us, expecting them to leave home—off to college, an apartment of their own, marriage. Then the grandbabies come and something happens. If we're not careful we offer ourselves as living sacrifices or oracles.

One all-star grandfather wanted his wife to go on a trip to Florida. "We can't," she said. "Marlis needs me to help with the baby. He's our first grandchild."

"If you think you're indispensable," he told her, "put your hand into a pail of water, and when you take it out, see how big a hole you leave."

His wife blinked, considered her options, and packed for Florida. She had just chalked up a few points toward being an all-star grandparent.

Reach for
the Hearing Aids

Wendy watched her mother bathe her new baby brother. Then she helped pat him dry and powder his velvety skin. While her mother fed him, Wendy sat close by.

The baby was a marvel, but he took up so much time. When he cried and turned all red, Wendy stopped her ears. She couldn't shut him off like television.

After her mother put the baby in the crib, Wendy said, "Now will you play house with me?"

"First let's clean the bathroom and bake some cookies. Grandma is coming over to see the baby." Her mother hugged Wendy, so she felt happy again.

When grandmother arrived she kissed Wendy and said, "Where is that wonderful boy? I can't wait to hold him."

Wendy and mother picked him up, wrapped in a

yellow blanket, and placed him in grandmother's arms.
"Oh, the little darling," she said. "Isn't he sweet?
Isn't he the most beautiful baby in the world?"

Wendy looked at her brother closely. Then she said,
"Have you ever seen a picture of the baby Jesus?"

The question hovered in the silence like a butterfly.
I don't know how that grandmother replied. I hope
she laid aside the baby and picked up Wendy. I hope
she adjusted her hearing aid and gave full attention to
her granddaughter.

Listening is one activity all-star grandparents develop.
From their earliest days children need to know that
grandparents are their best friends, their admirers.

When a sitter for young children is needed, grandparents may offer help. It's important to come equipped
with Mother Goose rhymes, songs, games, laughter, and
keen ears.

With little children, grandparents have a golden opportunity to talk about when mom or dad was small
or to tell Bible stories. Eager ears will want to hear
the sound-recording again and again.

With children in the early grades, grandparents can
give not only time and strength, but something of their
wisdom and philosophy of life based on Scripture,
prayer, obedience, honesty, and kindness.

As the children reach adolescence, we need to switch
off telling them what we know or what they should do.
It's time to hang up the transmitter and fine tune to
what they are saying or not saying.

As the Preacher wrote, "There's a time to keep

silence, and a time to speak." If we must talk, let's tell what the Lord has been doing for us. Wise grandparents keep silent on many counts, except for curiosity and praise.

How shall we listen when grandchildren fail to tell us anything or the conversation dangles?

Those who begin when grandchildren are babies learn to develop a good ear. By the time children reach adolescence, the grandparents are keen-eared, awake to what the youngsters are trying to say. On occasion grandchildren may seek wisdom, but as a rule both will be on a walkie-talkie basis—separated but able to get through to each other.

One grandfather told me, "I've learned that if I want my grandchildren to hear me, I'd better shut up. Forget about how it was in the good old days. Forget about giving advice, unless it's asked for. Since that's almost never, forget about giving advice."

Teachers, peers, parents, and people on television, transistor radio, the public address system—there's always somebody trying to tell children something. But with all the decibels, is anyone listening? Don't hop into every silence. Grandchildren need someone to be quiet with them. Later they may use a grandparent as a sounding board.

In the silence or at other times we need to review our own youth. A friend confides that whenever she expects to be with her high school grandchildren, she thinks seriously about her own teenage years.

"I try to remember how I felt at 15 or 17. What was

important to me? A date? New clothes? A job? Figuring out who I was? What the future held? Thoughts about death? Temptation?" She adds, "Poking into the past helps me push aside my tendency to moralize, even mental scolding."

One suggestion comes from a grandmother with three junior high grandchildren. "Grandparents should be particular about their appearance, especially if living alone with no one to check up on them. When I visited my family last fall," she says, "one of the children asked, 'Grandma, are you going to buy shiny white boots like Sandy's grandma and ride a bicycle?'

"I told them no, I wasn't going to buy shiny white boots and ride a bicycle like Sandy's grandmother. But even though my closet was full of functional clothing, I bought a sharp new outfit so my grandchildren would consider me up-to-date."

Whenever she visits her son's home, one woman makes a point of watching a television program or two with her grandchildren. Listening to their records and checking out the books they read also pay off. Future shock is already invading our ordered lives.

As we hearken to our grandchildren, whatever their age, if we put our whole mind to understanding them and their interests, we will find young people have much to teach us.

I remember when my brother's grandchildren and their parents from California visited me. The year before the boys had traveled in Europe where their

father, an authority on earthquake engineering, had attended an international seminar on seismology.

"I'd like to take you boys to the top of the IDS tower in Minneapolis," I said. "It's 770 feet high. Or did you go to the top of the Empire State Building?"

"No," Kevin said. "I've never been in the Empire State Building. The highest one I've been in is the Eiffel Tower in Paris."

Quickly I came down from the top of the IDS Building and said, "Tell me about it."

Once while we were baking cookies a granddaughter said to me, "I don't think I'll get married. If I did it would be just my luck to marry some hippie or drunk."

"No," I told her. "Perhaps even now the one you will marry is thinking about his future. I'm going to pray that God will help him be the best person he can be. And that you will be your best for him."

Her eyes shone. "You are, Grandma?"

"Don't be surprised," I added, "when God sends the right boy along."

The most popular grandparents have fun. They bring laughter to any situation. If within the realm of possibility, they get down on all fours and play horsie for the toddlers. They take grade-schoolers sliding or swimming or to the zoo. They're not above bribery, handing out occasional green stuff to a teenager whose allowance turns out to be inadequate that week.

Of course, in grave situations grandparents must stand firm for the principles of God. There are times when we can't help but speak out against sin and uphold family rules and traditions. Except for these encounters, a grandparent can learn to be, not the star, but the audience.

"Don't talk so much. You keep putting your foot in your mouth. Be sensible and turn off the flow!" (Prov. 10:19 LB). Reach for hearing aids. What we know and don't say may be more important than what we say.

Small Boats
and Big Seas

Practically all grandparents aspire to be top-level performers. The danger is that as we baby-sit, bestow gifts, feel love and concern for our grandchildren, we will interfere with their parents' rights.

Any grandparent who tries to interfere, criticize, or hand out advice will be accused of rocking the boat. It's hard to be a parent today. Our children need all the support we can give, not interference or criticism.

An old proverb reads: My boat is so small, and God's sea is so great. We are all small boats—parents, grandparents, and grandchildren, and in the face of life's demands we cry out for help.

From talking to other grandparents and observing myself, I have learned it's easy to assume that our many years as parents and our love for our children entitle us, when the grandbabies arrive, to speak from the platform of experience. Nothing could be further from reality.

It's up to parents to train, feed, be responsible for their children. Still, what grandparent hasn't itched to give advice when word comes, "Terry won't eat vegetables" or "Jeff refused to do his homework" or "Susie wants to marry this boy without a job."

Aren't grandparents qualified to offer counsel in such instances? After all, we've lived 50, 60, or 70 years— years of great change and innovation. We know a lot, don't we?

Besides, with God's unfailing help and in spite of mistakes on our part, we managed to rear some fine children. We have learned to synchronize our habits with the beat of life. What's wrong with speaking up?

We do indeed have experience and knowledge to impart. But there's a line drawn when it comes to teaching our children's children. It's time to forget such favorite parental topics as brushing teeth, table manners, unmade beds, and laziness. Instead we can teach skills that are peculiarly ours—organ playing, knitting, repairing cars, fishing. We can offer love and lobby for good relations with others, or for courage in the face of danger, or obedience to unchanging principles.

Assuming a child's parents do not forbid it, we can explain what it means to be a follower of the Lord Jesus Christ. We can pray and read the Bible with the children when they visit us. In the quietness of our hearts we can pray for them every day.

Some years ago I was invited to help out when the

fourth baby arrived in one family. I accepted with alacrity. Soon I found cleaning up the kitchen every evening after dinner occurred when I felt rather delicate, with my patience at zero.

One night I said, "Please let me wash the dishes without having to sing nursery rhymes and settle squabbles. I want to meditate."

"Of course," the parents said as they scooped up the babies and hooked the gate between kitchen and dining room.

While washing dishes, I talked to God about my inadequacy and the greatness of his sea. Forty-five minutes later when I joined the family, the kitchen was in order and I was remarkably refreshed.

I believe my grandmother knew her helplessness and prayed to God about the vastness of his sea.

She wore long skirts and a net collar around her throat. When, as a child, I visited her, she let me play in the flour stored in a bin that tipped out from under her work table. With washed hands and little cups and spoons, I dredged around in the flour, listening to my grandmother's gentle voice and the thump of the bread dough as she kneaded.

How unsanitary! How delightful! I was permitted to do something that would have been illegal at home with four children under eight. Perhaps that's why I remember the flour bin and other instances of my grandmother's love and indulgence those summers I visited her.

What I am also grateful for is that she taught me

unchanging principles of right and wrong, repeated from time to time in her letters through the years. She had high hopes for her grandchildren—small boats in a wide sea—and she prayed for them.

Teaching such principles is not easy when grandparents rarely see their grandchildren. One woman's son lived with his family in distant countries for years at a time. They were almost strangers whenever they met.

Yet she determined to draw them to her with love and faith. She wrote each child regularly, whether answers reached her or not, relating examples of God's providence in her life.

As the children grew older their unorthodox ways and their disregard for church distressed her. Still she prayed for each grandchild day after day. Years later a letter reached her from a grandson stationed in Turkey.

Dear Gram:

I want to tell you about the most wonderful thing that has ever happened to me. I have accepted Jesus Christ as my Savior.

It is ironic that I had to come to a country where less than one percent of the population is Christian to realize I had been running away from God all my life.

I was not very happy with my life, and was searching but didn't know for what. As you well know my religious training up to now has been very scant.

One of the men I work with, a Christian, noticed how depressed I was and talked to me over a period of weeks. Then he took me to a Bible study group. They were studying John 14. I read it over and over and two weeks later I turned my life over to Jesus Christ. I now realize that God had a purpose in sending me to Turkey, and I am studying the Bible. Gram, I thought you'd like to know.

Love,
Randy

If God sees fit to send a grandchild into storm-tossed seas, keep on praying. It may be that deliverance is at hand.

Often in our littleness, faced with God's magnitude, we wonder if he will hear our prayers for a grandchild in deep water. Or we are puzzled because the answer is so long delayed or does not coincide with our desires.

My friend Winola has a word of caution about prayer. "I put my burdens in the lap of the Lord," she says. "But I made a mistake. I picked them up again." In such times we need to pray in the words of the songwriter, "Teach me the patience of unanswered prayer."

From their grandchildren's birth through their adulthood, grandparents make frequent use of prayer. And since, as philosopher Joseph Joubert says, "children have more need of models than critics," grandparents spend extra time praying for themselves, that they will be worthy examples.

Apprentice Grandparents

Four days after the birth of our first child, anxiety settled down on my shoulders like a heavy woolen cape. Parental training classes were almost unknown then. So were paperbacks on baby care.

How would I ever get through this one? The formula? The bath? What if he cried and wouldn't stop? On top of those nagging doubts, I felt overwhelmed at what stretched ahead for my husband and me. God had put into our arms a new little babe with an immortal soul to train and rear to responsible manhood. We'd never make it without God's help.

Older grandparents will recall with me that new mothers stayed flat in bed in the hospital for 10 days. Then they went home with instructions to "feed him every four hours." More than one young mother wished for a grandmother who would come out of the bush and be handy.

Even young grandmothers realize, if they take a refresher course, that what they know about baby care is old-fangled. Mothers today are walking around the hospital the same day the baby is born and back home in three or four days.

Young parents have attended classes and read books on parenting. They have received solid training on how to feed, bathe, and dress their babies. This gives them confidence to be in charge. A grandmother in the house may be in the way.

Yet parents still need God's help, plus gentleness, love, and wisdom. So do apprentice grandparents, and all the rest of us. No matter how well-prepared we think we are to take on the joys and responsibilities of being grandparents, when the time comes we're in for a few shocks. It's nip and tuck whether we'll prove successful!

What are a few suggestions for grandparents serving their apprenticeship?

Don't front-page the news until the parents-to-be are ready to have it headlined. Remember the coming event belongs first of all to them.

Don't smother them with attention and offers of help. Most modern parents are knowledgeable and confident. In the hospital, admire the baby and stay away from the couple and their callers.

Don't offer advice—no matter how experienced you think you are, no matter how sure you are your advice would be helpful.

One of my young friends declares, "My grandmother

tried to take over when I was born. She honestly thought my mother wasn't capable of bringing up children. By barging in, my grandmother made a lifetime enemy of my mother."

No grandmother in her right mind would knowingly make that mistake.

Less confident young mothers may welcome help. Grandparents can let the young people know they are ready if needed, then stand back and let the new parents take the initiative.

After all those "don'ts," what can grandparents *do?*

Nine months is a long wait. Grandparents can think of ways to brighten or shorten the waiting. Many young couples starting out feel the pinch of today's economy. One seminarian's wife, soon to be a mother, stopped me at church and said, "My parents sent plane tickets for us to come home for Christmas." The glow on her face was unforgettable.

Although not everyone can afford such brighteners, we can manage other thoughtful gifts. Tickets for two to a concert or dinner in an elegant restaurant, something glamorous for the mom-to-be to wear the final weeks, or an extravagant and fashionable gift for the baby will shorten the time.

After the baby's birth, if the couple are willing, try to see that the new mom comes home to a clean house, with washing done and freezer stocked. Cook a bang-up meal for the new father. This may be his last chance to relax for a while.

When the expected baby is not the first in the family, grandparents can care for the other children, a service that is rarely turned down.

While waiting, grandparents can visit the library and check out modern books on child care, or ask the mom-to-be what books she suggests. Tell her, "It's been a long time since I cared for a tiny baby, and I want to be ready if I'm asked to baby-sit."

The special qualities grandparents have to offer come from having faced innumerable emergencies and crises, and the strength they derive from faith in God.

Most parents want to train their own children with no interference from the older generation. A few years ago a wise man said, "The home is the first training school in behavior or misbehavior, and parents are a child's first teachers."

If grandparents back up the young people's efforts with approval and support, they may also find opportunities to remind them of the wisdom of Solomon: "Teach a child to choose the right path, and when he is older he will remain upon it" (Prov. 22:6 LB).

One grandmother of several says, "We pray for the parents. They are rearing their children in a world of growing godlessness. They need God's help."

Her husband adds, "We try to praise the things our kids do right, including innovations, and we try to keep mum about their failures."

A father, mother, two children and their grandmother visited a neighbor. The children played in a corner with blocks and games while the grown-ups talked. When it was time to go, the grandmother said, "Shouldn't the children pick up the toys?"

"Yes," the mother said. The children did pick up the toys, for they had been well-trained. How much better if the grandmother had kept mum. Afterward she might have told the children, "I was proud of you, the way you picked up the toys."

New grandparents sometimes write a letter to the grandbaby. Had I thought to do that when my grandchildren were born, the letter might have read something like this:

Dear Baby:

After peeking at you wrapped in a pink blanket in your basket behind glass, I agree with everything your parents say about you. You are beautiful, and you look like your father's baby picture. You also have a strong pair of lungs.

You have been born into a Christian family, the fruit of your parents' love for each other. They want the best for you, and so do I. They will teach you about Jesus, I know. Jesus referred to Christians as lambs, and he called himself the Lamb of God.

Long ago William Blake wrote a poem called "The Lamb."

Little Lamb, who made thee?
Dost thou know who made thee?
. . . .
Little Lamb, I'll tell thee.
Little Lamb, I'll tell thee:
He is callèd by thy name,
For he calls himself a Lamb.

He is meek and he is mild,
He became a little child.
I a child, and thou a lamb,
We are called by his name.
Little Lamb, God bless thee!
Little Lamb, God bless thee!
Dear grandchild, I hope your parents will sometimes call you "little lamb." I pray that Jesus, our tender Shepherd, will bless you, and you will early learn to follow him.

Love from
Your Grandmother

When children are born into the world they have much to learn. So do parents. So do grandparents.

Creepers, Leapers, and Knee-Sitters

At the post office I held open the heavy door. Out lurched a toddler, with her mother clutching her hand. Putting one short leg in front of the other, the child looked up at me, smiled, and jabbered.

I didn't need her mother to interpret what the child was saying: "Look! I can walk."

"You can walk," I said in appreciation. "Aren't you a dolly?"

"Oh, yes," her mother said ruefully. "She insists on going it alone. Won't let me pick her up. Thirty-five hours in the day would be about right."

The child tugged at her mother to keep going.

"What you need is a grandmother," I said. The mother nodded and took off after her child.

Mothers of babies and toddlers must be the most overworked minority in the land. They are on 24-hour alert, week after week. Most of them are eager to

export a toddler on occasion, if a loving grandparent issues an invitation.

When one grandmother welcomed her two-year-old grandson, complete with baggage, she asked her daughter, "How long will you be gone?"

The mother replied with a grin, "Till he's 18."

They need help, those young mothers.

One way is to support parents with approval and concern. A young mother I talked to said, "It really hurts when the grandparents aren't interested in the kids. I'm glad they're having a good time in Arizona or Florida, but it helps if they remember water pipes are freezing in Minnesota, and the kids probably have chicken pox."

We also need to upgrade our knowledge of danger spots for creepers and climbers—electric cords, knives, glassware, and household cleaning supplies. We can be open to suggestions from a young mother, and perhaps put breakables out of reach.

Some grandparents have firm ideas about not helping with small grandchildren. "I'm delighted to be a grandmother, and I carry the baby's pictures in my purse, but I never intend to be a baby-sitter." Hearing those words of a new grandmother made me feel a little sorry for her.

Grandfathers too may be reluctant baby-sitters. They'll never go wild over a grandbaby, right? Wrong. Grandbabies trap grandfathers, as well as grandmothers, for life.

Perhaps I'm more blessed than some in my children

and grandchildren. I would be the first to say so. I think grandparents are the losers when they overlook baby-sitting—on a free-lance basis.

After a stint I was often tired enough to go to bed for several days, or I picked up a child's cold that laid me low for a week. But I wouldn't exchange those volunteer baby-sitting hours for anything.

From experience with 10 grandchildren, I'd say baby-sitting is one way to rate. Besides, grandchildren keep us laughing. To ordinary occurrences they bring joy and playfulness that rub off on us.

Baby-sitting is a way to watch a child's personality unfold, as body, mind, and spirit grow. By example and words we can speak to them of our faith in God. Baby-sitting is a way to lay the foundation for a lifetime relationship.

Once, baby-sitting for three I felt exhausted and my patience was wearing thin. The children were quarrelsome and in need of diversion. I had run out of tricks, and their mother wasn't due home for another hour or two.

"Come," I said. "You need to work off steam. See if you can do my exercises." Together we did half a dozen grandmotherly exercises, leaving me puffing and the children warming up.

"Grandma," Sharon said, "can you do this?" She flipped over and stood on hands and head. Although I lost the contest, I won back a cheery outlook for the rest of the afternoon, while the children worked out a circus performance in the middle of the living room.

Another time, in the absence of Doug's parents, his grandmother was in charge. The older children prepared for bed, but Doug, only five, needed a story, a drink of water, prayers said, a drink of water, a little bedside talk, and a drink of water.

Grandmother's patience gave out. "That's enough fooling around, young man. You settle down."

Doug howled lustily. "I'm afraid. I'm afraid." His grandmother told him there was nothing to be afraid of, that she was just outside his door. Finally sleep took over.

The next day his grandmother reproached Doug. "You acted babyish last night."

"Oh, Grandma," he said, "that was just a practical joke."

Hiding her chuckle, she replied, "See that you don't repeat that joke tonight."

In between baby-sitting assignments, my daughter and daughter-in-law kept me informed of their children's accomplishments, bright sayings, lost teeth, and stitched cuts. They never took advantage of my willingness to baby-sit.

Others may have to take precautions to protect themselves. Esther had finished the breakfast dishes and was straightening the living room when her daughter Jan called.

"Mother, would you like a baby-sitting job?"

"Anytime but tomorrow afternoon. I have a luncheon," Esther replied. "I would love Glen for an afternoon."

After a pause Jan said, "I mean sort of a permanent baby-sitting job, like about a year." Then the words rushed out. "Everything costs so much and Steve says we're falling behind, and we want to save for Glen's education, and I need new shoes, and we were thinking if I went back to work for a year, we'd catch up."

"Well!" Esther said. "I'm not as strong as I used to be. Besides, your father wants me to go west with him on a business trip. I love little Glen, but I don't believe I could take care of him day after day."

"You're not that old," Jan said.

"Once you go back to work you'll probably want to continue. I was reading the other day that the ideal arrangement for working mothers is for the baby to be in a family with other little children." Esther paused, choosing her words with care. "You must know some young mother at home with children who could use extra money." Then Esther added, "Remember, I'm always available for emergencies."

Bravo for Esther!

Besides safeguarding their rights, grandparents need to cut rules for grandchildren to a minimum.

Every other weekend the caretakers in a large apartment complex post a sign on their door that reads, "Do not disturb. This is our weekend off." Something about that sign tempts me to lift the knocker and let it fall with a loud clack. Is it the same, I wonder, with children? When they hear, "Don't do this" and "Don't do that" so often, do they think, "Maybe I will"?

A youngish grandmother told me, "We have a few

big rules when the grandchildren visit at our lake cabin. Nobody hops into the boat unless Grandpa is there. Nobody goes on the dock or walks into the lake unless Grandpa is there.

"I bought a terry tablecloth, so it doesn't matter what they spill. If they want to eat their mashed potatoes with their fingers, I let them. After all, how many teenagers still eat mashed potatoes with their fingers?"

She must be a grandmother who's fun to be with.

Keeping rules few and simple makes it easier to insist on obedience and discipline. No one jumps up and down on beds or sofas at Grandma's house—not if she knows it.

Often I've heard "Mommy lets us" or "Mommy doesn't do it that way."

"That's a good way too," I point out, "but at Grandma's house we do it this way."

Four-year-old Rosemary was about as practical as they come. Once at the table her younger sister Judy rebelled at some edict. Rosemary, waving her fork in a forthright manner, said, "Yah, Judy, at Grandma's house we do it her way." This basic rule helps avoid clashes. Grandparents need not spoil grandchildren or give in to their demands to win their affection.

If grandchildren visit regularly, invest in a second-hand crib to be sold when the children no longer nap.

Stock a box or shelf with enticing toys and games. When our grandchildren were creepers and leapers, my husband brought home a grotesque red monkey, one no grandmother would select. But it fascinated the

children. Not long ago one of the teens asked, "Whatever happened to the red monkey?"

Begin a children's bookshelf too, starting with Mother Goose and picture books for the tiniest ones. Add "two-lap" books that grandparents read over and over, and a Bible story book.

One grandmother confined to a wheelchair in her son's home looked forward to the hour just before dinner when her granddaughter sat on a footstool beside her and together they looked at picture books, learned scripture verses, and sang happy songs.

Granted, baby-sitting little ones is not exactly reclining in a La-Z-Boy chair, and knee-sitters are heavy to hold.

Granted, we grandparents walk a tightrope between longing to know our grandchildren and protecting our own rights.

Granted, the path of grandparents may be lined with irritations, jolts, and disappointments. Fringe benefits, though, far outweigh all these. And I can give grandparents a promise, not original with me. "The steadfast love of the Lord is from everlasting to everlasting upon those who fear him, and his righteousness to children's children" (Ps. 103:17).

Looking for God's Autograph

One summer night when I was a child, we had been playing tag. Hot and breathless, we flung ourselves on the grass to cool off. A grownup on the porch said, "Look at the moon." High in the purple expanse, it seemed very far away. "How big do you think the moon is?" the grownup asked. "The size of an orange? Or a dining room table?"

The question wasn't settled that night. But many times since I have looked at the moon and wondered how big God made it. When space exploration answered the question I felt wistfulness for a tug of imagination now replaced by scientific knowledge.

It took imagination as well as courage—and faith in God—for men to reach the moon. In our complex world we need men and women of courage and imagination and faith.

We can help our grandchildren understand, as Coleridge says, that "In today already walks tomorrow." Our grandchildren will be the workers, craftsmen, inventors, teachers, parents, and leaders of the future.

Growing up in a computerized world, they need to take time to look at God's creation. As we help open their eyes to his miracles, to his handiwork in commonplace things, children will not only develop imagination. They will also learn reverence for God. And reverence for God is the foundation for becoming good custodians of our world.

A grandfather I admire says, "We help the kids see that all the important inventions have not already been made. From the time they were little we encouraged them to use their imagination."

Children are light-hearted in imagining. "The caterpillar giggles when it wiggles," goes a nursery song. And the children giggle at the idea.

A little girl visiting her grandmother cried, "Ouch!" When her grandmother asked what happened, the child replied, "I scratched my arm on your cat."

After a freezing rain that hung icicles on fences and trees, a child riding with his grandfather said, "Look, Grandpa, the stop sign has whiskers."

Children can look for the imprint of God as they trudge through woods, splash in lakes, crane necks at snow-topped mountain and star-splintered sky, in all seasons, night and day.

Once as we sat at breakfast in a cabin in Crow Wing County, Minnesota, my husband helped our

grandchildren see the wonder and humor of one of God's creatures.

A large blue heron, in search of food, awkwardly waded along the shore. Sitting still so no movement would frighten it away, we watched. We heard the schlip-schlip of water each time the bird lifted a pipe-stem leg and set its foot down again. Abruptly the heron thrust its beak into the water, caught a fish, then spread its huge wings, mounting into the sky.

"Look," the children's grandfather said, as the bird tucked its long legs under its body. "The heron has retractable landing gear."

With glee they echoed, "Retractable landing gear."

For her grandchildren, a Minnesota poet marked a nature trail in the woods near the family's vacation spot. She identified and labeled hundreds of wild flowers, plants, and shrubs along the trails. She marked the entrance to a fox's den, a woodchuck's hole, a bee-hive, and other signs of God.

Grandparents can unveil the marks of God in common things in the city as well. We can point out the flight of robins and swallows across traffic-clogged streets, the taste of fresh snowflakes on the tongue, or the explosion of God's power as lightning stabs the sky.

While looking for signposts of God, grandparents should never hesitate to say, "I don't know." Children and the rest of us need things we can't explain or understand to show us how small we are and how enormous God is.

We have to be careful not to do all the talking, all the explaining. Let the grandchildren say what they see or think. Prod them to use imagination. Wait for them to ask, "Did God use an airplane to hang the stars in the sky?" or "How does a baby bird learn to fly?"

Children educate us in surprising ways. Seeing through a child's eyes takes away the dimness of our own. What has become ordinary is full of wonder. God's autograph stands out in capital letters.

> God moves in a mysterious way
> His wonders to perform;
> He plants his footsteps in the sea,
> And rides upon the storm.
>
> Blind unbelief is sure to err,
> And scan his work in vain.
> God is his own Interpreter,
> And He will make it plain.
>
> William Cowper

As we slow down the days grow shorter. Still there's time to take a grandchild on a walk to look for works of God in the world around us. There's time to write distant grandchildren about landmarks and secret signs of God and stir up their imagination.

Looking for the miracles of God in everyday life will develop our grandchildren's imagination and increase their faith in God—preparation for future leadership.

Never a
Dull Moment

A traveling companion and I once visited Beatrix Potter's home near Sawrey, England, where she wrote and illustrated her famous *The Tale of Peter Rabbit.* She also wrote other enchanting stories about frogs and mice and kittens, who have human characteristics and meet grave problems which they struggle to overcome.

When a movie of *The Tale of Peter Rabbit,* filmed in England, arrived in our city, my friend said, "Let's go and relive our trip." She added, "I want to take my little grandson."

Inside the darkened theater we settled down to enjoy scenes of England and Peter Rabbit. Into the silence my friend's three-year-old grandson asked in a voice that carried well, "Grandma, what channel is this?"

Although accustomed to television, the child had never been in a movie theater before. Older children too are caught in the spell of television.

In her book *The Plug-In Drug,* Marie Winn declares, "Without a doubt the availability of television as a child-rearing tool has reduced parents' immediate need to know their children well." As a result some children don't confide in parents as often or openly as did children a generation ago.

This is not a chapter on the demerits of television viewing, but a plea for grandparents to tune into the thoughts, fears, and feelings of their grandchildren and help them discover what they are missing while spending hours in the dark watching TV. We can show grandchildren how all look and no play puts the lid on their inventiveness and castle-building.

Child psychologists and teachers suggest that, as much as possible, an adult view TV programs with children to explain violence and frightening situations or even to switch off the set.

Grandparents then need to be ready with replacements. Providing substitute activities that help children use their imagination and skill may not be easy, especially in the children's home, if they are used to regular programs. With ingenuity, though, grandparents will find ways to keep the children busy and out of mischief. A grandparent who arrives equipped with a bag of props soon learns children often choose to be where the attention and activity is.

At the grandparents' house where the pace is slower, games, photos, books, and curios may beckon the child. Along with other grandparents, I have found that, with things to do and the warmth of attention, children rarely ask to watch TV.

Practical skills

Resourcefulness can color such activities as baking cookies, building a stool, weeding a garden, repairing an electrical switch or cord.

One man, walking in woods or parks with his grand-children, taught them to identify birdcalls. He imitated the nuthatch, purple finch, oriole, and others. The rest of us, less talented, might invest in a record of bird calls, or borrow one from the library.

Another man took his grandchildren fishing, some-times in the creek up in the woods, sometimes near the beaver dam. He taught them how to dig for worms, pull one out of the tin can, stick the worm, and let it wiggle on the hook. He taught them how to handle the cane pole, twice as tall as a boy, and not to fling the baited hook into a leafy green bush or tree—or worse, hook the arm or bare foot of another fisherman.

Other men introduce their grandchildren to fishing by way of a 40-horsepower motor and artificial bait. As the boat cuts the water on the way to the fishing spot, grandkids yell, "Go faster, Grandpa!" Part of the fun of fishing is learning to clean and fry the fish.

Games and puzzles

Invest in some old-fashioned board games: Caroms, Flinch, Chinese Checkers, Pit, Scrabble, and one or two

newer games. And be sure to buy several puzzles! Children love putting them together—and you can help.

I have a colorful 600-piece puzzle of the state of Minnesota. We bring it out on holidays and the whole family sets to work putting the pieces together. The puzzle also holds the interest of grandchildren on short visits. We talk about various towns, lakes, and places we have seen and others we would like to see.

Family treasures

One of the pastimes my grandchildren enjoyed when small was to look at my bell collection. They unwrapped each little glass, ceramic, or brass bell, rang it, and set it out on the dining table to admire. The story or history of the various bells fascinated them. In imagination they took off to another time or country. Occasionally they chose a bell to take home for their own.

Old watches, jewelry, dishes, or other treasures, books, and photo albums take on meaning for children when grandparents explain their history.

But children soon tire of hearing only about the past. They are living today and dreaming of tomorrow.

Scripture, hymns, poetry

Bible verses, hymns, and great poetry can be memorized while working together. A junior high girl says that as a child visiting her grandparents she often learned the words of hymns. Once when she felt tempted to do wrong, the words "and shield my soul from sin" came to her mind. She couldn't remember the rest of the hymn but those few words were enough to help her escape.

Children can make posters and banners using scripture verses. Bright banners made of coarse material with letters cut from contrasting colored flannel and pasted on provide ways for a child to be original.

Manners

More easily caught than taught, "manners are the happy way of doing things," Emerson said. When grandchildren visit, we have opportunity to show by our example. Good manners sometimes require self-control in not saying what we really think, but rather waiting for the child to grow.

Castles in the air

As we talk about the children's best qualities, talents, and ways to develop them, we encourage dreams about the future.

Discipline

When I grew tired caring for grandchildren who were mischievous, I tended to scold in stereo, which was a poor example of public relations. One day I learned a lesson from Dan and his mother. He handed her a holder he had made, shaped like a Ping-Pong paddle.

"Here," he said. "Save your voice." The holder had a slot to receive large-lettered signs such as "Stop," "Danger," "Yield." Dan had the right idea.

As any experienced grandparent knows, we need to find energy outlets for school-age children or they'll take out their feelings on each other. "I'm going to clobber him" means the child needs something to do. In a fight between children, grandparents should remain as neutral as possible, though a little judicial intervention may be in order. In a tense situation one grandmother says, "I look for something to laugh about with the child. You change things more quickly with laughter than with scolding."

A teacher of young children says, "When a child is in trouble with others, ask him to teach a skill to another child."

As someone once said, "Children are always a handicap to grown-ups who want to lead a dull life." Grandparents who enjoy the enthusiasm and brightness of young life, who bring love and resourcefulness to whatever time they spend with their grandchildren, will find life is never dull when they are together.

Reading

Grandparents can bring back the "children's hour" by reading aloud. With an arm encircling one child, or sitting close when more are listening, we can introduce children to worthwhile books. (A partial list of books I have read to grandchildren appears below.)

As a child I read fairy books, the *Red, Yellow,* and *Blue Fairy Books,* plus Hans Christian Andersen's fairy tales and *The Arabian Nights.* I wouldn't have missed them for anything.

By the time my grandchildren were interested, authorities had deleted parts of well-known fairy tales to soften their impact on children. No longer did the wolf swallow Red Riding Hood and her grandmother. Nor did the woodcutter kill the wolf. Too violent! No longer were Cinderella's wicked stepsisters banished.

The heart, the point, the excitement of fairy tales had been what Bruno Bettelheim calls "bowdlerized." While reading his book *The Uses of Enchantment*, I was heartened to learn that he, a psychologist for disturbed children, recommends well-known fairy tales to help children discover the meaning of themselves and their struggles.

But it's the old fairy tales he means, with all the excitement of a hero facing a villain, struggling to overcome evil. Such fairy tales, Bettelheim says, help children confront their own battles.

Grandparents can be ready to talk about what might be fearful in the fairy tale, so the children learn by discussion. Some of the thrilling biographies in the Bible are also violent and may need explaining.

Books for grandchildren's shelf

A Bible story book

Bemelmens, Ludwig, *Madeline* and *Madeline's Rescue*

Burton, Virginia, *Mike Milligan and His Steam Shovel*

Carroll, Lewis, *Alice's Adventures in Wonderland*

De Regniers, Beatrice Shenk, and Haas, Irene, *A Little House of Your Own*

Lewis, C. S., *The Chronicles of Narnia*

Mother Goose

Potter, Beatrix, *The Tale of Peter Rabbit* and *The Tale of Mr. Jeremy Fisher*

Saint-Exupery, Antoine de, *The Little Prince*

White, E. B., *Charlotte's Web*

Wilder, Laura Ingalls, Little House books

Yates, Elizabeth, *Carolina's Courage*

A Bar of Yellow Soap

One seldom sees a bar of yellow laundry soap today. Grandparents will recall it had one purpose besides cleansing the family wash and scrubbing hands which had brushed against poison ivy. It was also used as a mouth cleanser.

I remember how I learned about yellow soap. I was a child playing with others in the alley back of our house when I first heard four-letter words. The words, shouted with wild freedom, sounded like fun.

Trying them out in the warmth of our kitchen, I found that the excitement of saying what the others had said was cancelled by having my mouth washed out with soap. Parents then had a straightforward response to profanity and obscenity. Bad words called for that bar of yellow soap.

Many raised thus join me in being disgusted and uncomfortable with the increasing use of filthy and debasing language in public places or in small groups. In films, on radio and TV, in books, magazines, and newspapers, the names of God and Jesus Christ are debased and defiled. Vulgar and filthy words are tossed about like gum wrappers.

A television program I sometimes watch jolted me the other evening. The charming wife in the comedy found her husband's behavior so annoying she stamped her foot and took God's name in vain, swearing at her husband twice.

Adding to my disgust was a news item in the morning paper with the caption, "Court says seven dirty words are permissible on airwaves." The words had previously been banned.

About the same time I sat as a guest at a university writers' conference listening to three authors of best-sellers. In response to a question from the floor the young woman on the panel defended her use of scatological words in her book. She asked the audience's pardon, then cited and stood firm on her use of the words.

Since profanity and obscenity flourish in many best-selling books, young readers are often exposed to such words. Some have never learned, or don't care, that blasphemy breaks one of God's Ten Commandments and that filthy talk is condemned in the Bible. Both profanity and four-letter words offend good taste and morals. Each generation of children hears the offensive words more and more frequently.

To offset this grandparents might follow the method

of one woman who taught her grandchildren the words of Philippians 4:8 before they went to school. She assigned each phrase of the scripture to a pudgy finger—"whatever is true, whatever is honest. . . ."

In defense of profane and obscene words, a psychologist declares that the user is "letting off steam." But there are better ways to open the petcock.

My mother had one. After the bar of yellow soap, she offered me substitute words. Her habit of using polysyllabic words—folderol, highfalutin, atrocious, idiosyncrasy, flabbergasted, and many others—meant we children learned the meaning of the words and used them ourselves. There were no limits to the music, mystery, and power of the words we heard while growing up.

The dictionary contains words that can release pent-up feelings, words that carry more clout than does profanity, words that set the mind to thinking along constructive lines.

Although profane and filthy expressions are often the result of anger and lack of emotional control, they are frequently a careless habit, an attempt to conform to the pack's language. At least I like to think that was so with one teenage mother. We sat in the lounge of a garage waiting for our cars to be serviced. The young mother grew impatient with her toddler's climbing on chairs and the table and ripping magazines apart.

"Lisa," she yelled, calling the child an obscene word. Then she picked up the little girl and tickled her. It was plain the young mother had never learned the power of polysyllabic words, nor the offense to others of shouted obscenity.

Grandparents can influence children by using unfamiliar and appropriate words, at the same time explaining their meaning.

A child ran screaming to his grandmother who was baby-sitting. "She called me a bad name," he reported. "Susie said I'm ob—obnoshish." He didn't understand he was growing up in a family where vocabulary was rolled around on tongues.

The grandmother picked up the little boy in her arms. "That wasn't kind of Susie," she said. "You're not obnoxious. You're lovable."

When seven-year-old Susie came in, she said, "Grandma, he was telling stories about monsters as if they were true. He's just preposterous."

The four-year-old howled again. "She's calling me a bad name."

Grandmother wiped away tears, offered milk and cookies, and then explained the difference between bad words and big ones. She also helped the child pronounce *obnoxious,* handing him a weapon for some future occasion.

Jill showed her vocabulary didn't draw on coarse words to get her meaning across. Her friend Debbie had walked home from school with her. Over a snack at the kitchen table, they talked about a third girl.

"I thought Sheryl was coming too," Debbie said. Then she labeled the absent girl with a filthy word.

"You can't depend on her," Jill said. "One minute

she's coming, the next she's not. She's a flibbertigibbit."

Debbie blinked. "What's that?" Then she whispered, "Is it a bad word?"

"No." Jill giggled. "It means what Sheryl is. She's flighty."

I'm not sure whether Jill and Debbie had tried very hard to persuade Sheryl to join them. But Jill knew a polysyllabic word that fit Sheryl's behavior.

I questioned the parents of one family of teenagers. "What do you do when your young people use profane or obscene words?"

"We forbid them to use such talk in our home," they replied. "We don't allow pseudo-profanity either —words like Gol-darn, holy smoke, or jeez."

Perhaps we can't do much to sway the majority of those who carelessly use such language, but we can uphold standards in our own home and with our own grandchildren.

The dictionary classes profane and obscene words as expletives or fillers, words used to fill a vacancy. Profanity and obscenity both reveal poverty of language. Choosing unusual words from the hundreds of thousands listed in the dictionary is more fun.

Put-Downs
and Buildups

Two little girls hopped off the bus lugging their traveling bags for a weekend at Grandma's. After they unpacked their clothes, one said, "Grandma, what does Hallelujah mean?"

"It means praise the Lord," Grandma replied.

"Well, that's what Nancy said when we told her we were coming here for three days."

"That's what I say too," Grandma said, hugging the little girls, while they laughed together. Their older sister had put them down, but their grandmother used the same phrase to build them up.

Being put down by older brothers and sisters is a common experience for many children. We may think, "Little people, little troubles." But to children their troubles are big: parents scolding, teachers piling on homework, brothers and sisters out-performing them, friends ridiculing them. Usually in any conflict with parent or teacher, the adult wins and the child loses.

A woman whose wisdom I respect notes, "Experience has taught me that the secret of understanding grandchildren is to listen and learn how they feel. That's why a put-down is so devastating. It strikes where feelings are."

A put-down is anything that makes a child feel stupid or inferior or the object of ridicule. Those in the early grades are just beginning to wonder about themselves, and sometimes they doubt their own worth. The feeling often persists through high school and into adulthood. Children of all ages need loving adult support and encouragement.

Increasingly support may be lacking. With the upsurge of divorce, many children are growing up in single parent homes. Since more and more mothers are working full time, children may be deprived of the close love and attention they need.

When grandparents fill in for absentee parents or when grandchildren visit, the challenge is how to grow close to them, understand their feelings, and build them up.

A grandfather plays a vital role with grandchildren, especially if their father is absent or missing. Using a notebook to record the story of his granddaughter's visits, one man made the child feel worthwhile. Before she could write he pulled her onto his lap and asked what she had been doing all day while he worked. Then he wrote a few sentences in the child's own words, dating each chapter of the story.

Some pages were tear-splashed, as when the puppy next door dashed into the street and a car ran over it. Other pages told of decorating Christmas cookies with grandmother, learning to knit, helping granddad build a snowman taller than the little girl. As she learned to write, the child set down her own record of what happened on her visits to her grandparents.

Years later the story book held rich meaning for her. "I always felt I was important to my grandfather," she said.

From the time my grandchildren were small I have kept a file folder for each one. Into the folder I slipped letters, handmade valentines, recital programs, achievements, honors. Now the folders remind me of how many milestones the children have passed.

In a desk in her living room, a woman keeps a small album of yearly school pictures of her grandchildren. The first thing the children do when they visit her is to inspect the albums and wonder whether their appearance has improved since last year.

Some childhood disappointments which may feel like put-downs are unavoidable, but we can help prepare children for them.

For several years 12-year-old Sue had grown too fast to wear the same winter coat two years. Each year her mother bought her a new coat. The year-old coat was handed down to Kay, and the two-year-old coat from Kay to Jeanie.

When their mother planned to take Sue shopping for a new coat, Kay said, "Jeanie and I never get new coats. As long as we have to wear Sue's old coats, why can't we go along and help pick out the new one?"

I don't believe they won out, but it was a problem to the younger girls. Later their grandmother smoothed their feelings of self-doubt by explaining that when the younger girls reached the fast-growing stage they too would have new coats.

As we drove to a committee meeting, a friend told me how the children in a family she knew were experts at putting others down. "All the way from the minister, teachers, the president, to parents, brothers, and sisters."

My friend was silent for a time. Then she said, "My psychology professor taught us that back of such behavior is self-doubt, lack of self-esteem, feelings of inadequacy, all adding up to a poor self-image."

If this is true, what can grandparents do when they hear their own grandchildren practicing the fault?

Years ago a minister's wife told me, "We teach our children never to criticize another child's looks or clothing, or their own, for that matter. Instead they should look for something to praise.

"God gave her that nose. God gave him those floppy ears. The Bible tells us we are made in God's image. Whether that image is spiritual or physical, the Word of God leaves no room for criticizing the appearance of others."

Grandparents can help children with a low opinion of their looks to accept what can't be changed, work on what can be improved, and highlight good qualities.

Perhaps the family finances can't be stretched far enough to cover a pair of name brand tennis shoes or the latest style in belts. Lack of stylish clothing should never be cause for a put-down.

The only thing anyone has a right to disapprove of in another is poor behavior—a child's spiteful words, jealous or dishonest acts.

Wise grandparents never compare one child with another, in the same family or a cousin's. They help children see themselves as special persons with God-given capabilities for right now and in the future.

All-star grandparents never ask questions or pry into the child's family affairs. Anything told in confidence will never be revealed by the grandparents.

Music and laughter also help a child forget feelings of failure. A man told me that while he visited in his granddaughter's home he learned how music could overcome a put-down.

He had finished the last bite of a piece of delicious apple pie. Turning to his granddaughter he said, "I suppose you are beat from preparing that good dinner. It's not easy with two kids in school and two under-foot."

His granddaughter laughed. "It does feel good just to sit and relax." The children had been excused and were playing on the floor. Then a scream pierced the after-dinner lull.

"She's a baby," one child shouted. "She doesn't know how to play like a kid."

"I'm not a baby," the little sister wailed.

"Come," their mother said, picking up the toddler and leading the three-year-old by the hand. "Let's sing." She settled the four children around her on the piano bench. For a while she played and helped the children sing happy action songs, teaching them it was more fun to sing together than call names.

Lacking a piano or the ability to play children's songs, a grandparent can use action records or hymns, singing with the children. The habit of singing down doubts, fears, and insecurity will stay with them a lifetime.

Some children react negatively to out-and-out praise. "You keep telling me how great I am," one boy told his mother in a fit of depression. "I'm not the best in math. I don't make all the touchdowns."

When we cheer or clap for a child's successful efforts —a home run, a prize-winning poster, Boy Scout awards, a top piano solo—we're not praising the performance so much as the effort expended by the child. We feel lifted up ourselves by the winner's success.

Children need to know they are loved even if they don't accomplish great deeds, even if they fall flat.

When grandchildren stumble or fail, grandparents can build them up. "So you failed the spelling test. I'm sorry. The words are hard. Next time I know you'll practice more." Or, "So you made a big mistake. I don't like that, but I love you."

It's not necessary that children win every contest. The main thing is that they compete with themselves.

Are they doing better today than a week ago or a month ago?

Put-downs or criticism teach a child to be critical. Praise for wobbly towers of blocks and tied shoelaces, for attempts to build birdhouses and bake chocolate cakes, for kindness and honesty—such praise encourages children to have confidence.

Deserved applause with love is the kind of buildup every grandchild needs.

Cheering Section

Sitting in an armchair with an afghan over her knees, an 80-year-old grandmother said, "Praise the Lord, I raised my family before we ever heard of adoleskents." She was part of a three-generation family, and sometimes the youngest generation was beyond her ken.

Come on, Gram! Kids haven't changed that much. Call them guys and girls, teenagers, young people, or adolescents. We went from home-scissored hair and homemade dresses to boys with crew cuts and girls wearing their dad's white shirt. Straggly, greasy hair and dirty clothes gave way to carefully styled hair jean-clad neatness.

The appearance of those in their teens may have changed from time to time, but young people have always questioned, defied, resisted, griped, rebelled. They've always been subject to moodiness, self-doubt, and curiosity about new experiences. By turns they are noisy or secretive, emotionally high or depressed. They cry easily and worry about what others think of them.

Behind their erratic behavior is lack of self-confidence. As they pull away from childhood, pressures from all sides propel them toward adulthood. Some question authority, argue defiantly with parents, and ignore grandparents.

But not all young persons are hard to reach. Many grandparents I've talked to have retained close rapport with their teenage grandchildren. I know a number of young people who go to their grandparents for long talks and for help with difficult decisions.

But many young persons desperately need a cheering section. They need someone to hear them out, to encourage them, someone sensitive to their feelings.

One 15-year-old who confides in his grandfather says, "If I have a problem, I want to talk to somebody. My parents almost blow a fuse. They say, 'No. That's wrong.' They don't wait to hear my side. You'd think I'd totaled the car or something.

"I talk to my grandfather about what's giving me a bad time at school or home, and he listens all the way. He just says, 'Hmmm' or 'I see' or 'You don't say' till I'm finished.

"Last time he didn't give me any advice, just asked a few questions. Then he said, 'Seems to me a smart boy like you can work that out. Let's pray about it.' He treats me like an adult."

Psychologists tell us this is where friction builds.

Young people are pulling away from childhood and parents are not ready to let go.

It is true that parents can pave the way toward a loving relationship between children and grandparents. In turn grandparents can help young people appreciate their parents.

"Your father and mother are fine parents," a man told his 10th-grade granddaughter. "They work hard to do what's right for you. They want the best for you. You can be proud of them."

Not every young person struggles through the same pressures. Some have more than others. Some lash out and everybody knows about theirs. Others keep their troubles bottled. They are pushed to go to college, to experiment with the "new morality" (it isn't). They want to know about life and death and how they fit into the scheme of things. They want to know about scary things. And clinging to them like a huge cobweb is adult hopelessness which has been spinning off on them for years.

What a challenge confronts grandparents—to be a cheering section. To allow others to dress, act, and speak in ways that are different from ours is no easy task. But we can try even as we speak out against wrong and uphold values such as honesty, courage, and purity. And put in a commercial for God from time to time.

We can be good examples of a life lived in the power of the Son of God. We can let our grandchildren know

God answers prayer, that we've seen him work miracles through 40, 50, or 70 years.

It's important not to put the same book jacket on all young people, but to try to understand each one by listening to doubts and questions. Ask, "What bothers you most about this?" or "Are you scared?"

Grandparents can help young people discover their strengths and aptitudes. One boy, fretting under family pressure for him to go to college, told his grandfather, "All my dad says is to get an education, that I'll never be a success without a college degree. Maybe I don't want to be a success like my dad. I can't see much fun in what he does. He works in an office all week and plays golf on Saturdays."

The boy had just finished overhauling the engine of a secondhand car. Even his father admitted his son had done a first-rate job. We need college trained specialists in our complex society. But we also need trained technicians to repair our cars, washers, television sets, and plumbing.

If there's no question about the youth's readiness for college, the cost need not hold a young person back. There are scholarships, grants, and interest-free loans available. Others may do better if after high school they work for a spell and then return to school with new zest. For some high school graduates vocational training may be the answer.

Grandparents need to be sensitive to the feelings of young people. At the checkout counter I stood behind a youngish grandmother and a teenage boy.

"Here," she said, handing him two small packages. "Go next door and return these while you're waiting."

The boy looked into both packages. "No way," he said, leaving one package and setting off with the other.

"That age!" his grandmother remarked to me. "They're impossible. He wouldn't return that package because it's panty hose."

Minus score for grandma!

All-star grandparents, though they sometimes feel like they're standing up in a hammock, keep informed about revolutionary changes in acceptable behavior and existing temptations. When a young person is ready to talk, they are ready to answer. They give their approval when they can and, if not, a reason for their disapproval.

They haven't forgotten the attraction of sin in their own youth, and they are willing to admit the enticements of today's temptations—drink and drugs, gambling and pornography, sex without marriage.

The worst response would be for grandparents to approve such behavior. Just as fruitless would be to piously quote the Ten Commandments or deliver a sermon. Most teens are not sermon fans.

One morning I stood waiting for the bus at the transfer point, I noticed a young man in his late teens sobbing on the bench. Then he stood up, approached me, and asked if I had any Kleenex.

At first I wondered whether it was going to be a

purse-snatching. Then I opened my bag and handed him a wad of tissues.

"Is something troubling you?" I asked.

"You might say that," he replied, blowing his nose. "My girl friend and I have this apartment. We were each paying half the rent. Now it's time to pay again, and she left me. I don't know where she is." He sobbed again.

After a moment I said severely, "You should put your trust in God, not a person."

"You are so right, ma'am," he said. "Thank you for the Kleenex."

I had to admit I hadn't been prepared for that encounter. As grandparents we need to be as ready to back up our strong convictions with reasons as one woman was. I'll call her Mrs. Carlton.

Her senior high granddaughter had followed the crowd experimenting with the Commandments. Now, up to her pierced ears in trouble, she had come to her grandmother for help.

"At church they tell us Jesus is the answer. But most of the time he's only a word," the girl said. "How are you going to know whether you and a boy are right for each other without sleeping with him? All my friends are doing it, but when I do wrong things I feel bad inside."

Some grandmothers might have fainted, but not Mrs. Carlton, who said later, "I felt I had lived my whole 65 years just to answer that question."

She told the girl, "God will guide you with his eye and protect you if you stay within his eyesight."

The girl broke down and wept, then asked God's forgiveness, and made a U-turn in her behavior.

"From now on," her grandmother said, "you're not alone. I'll be praying for you. If you ever need help, ask me. More than that, the warm loving presence of the Savior will be with you."

Mrs. Carlton continued, "It takes more courage to hold out for marriage than to live with a man without marrying. The pact, the pledge is not the same, nor are the obligations. In marriage they are for a lifetime."

Dr. Armin Gesswein, conference speaker on prayer, once said, "When I search the Scriptures I am utterly amazed to find that everything God does is by prayer."

If we take time to consider the needs of grandchildren, then talk to God about them, he may intervene in their behalf. Or he may open our eyes to see how we can help.

Because of their years of living and trust in God, many grandparents help their grandchildren to a wholesome outlook toward marriage.

One time I talked to a church group of junior high girls. When prayer time came, several of the girls prayed that certain boys they liked would be interested in them. I could identify with those girls, remembering that I had held the same longings when I was a teenager. The difference was that at that time no girl would bring such a bold wish into the open. I loved those modern girls who were frank about their hopes. Afterward we talked about the importance of being where God could guide them.

Grandparents can stress that marriage as such should not be life's goal. Rather the goal might be marriage to a person, one the grandchild has learned to know trust, and respect.

"You're always optimistic," a young woman once told me. "Were you always that way?"

I chuckled. "Indeed not. I wasn't very likable when I was your age. I was selfish, wanted my own way, and easily discouraged."

"What happened?" she asked.

"A remodeling job. I turned my life over to God's Spirit for guidance. I still am selfish and discouraged at times—when I forget and try to direct my own life."

As grandparents make known their values, their stand on ethical questions, the importance of self-discipline, young people should see that someone who loves them has the courage to take a position. And that faith in God's power will help them over slippery places.

"It Matches Me!"

One Christmas morn four-year-old Cindy tugged the ribbons and bright paper from a box on her lap. Then she jumped up squealing with delight. "It matches me." She held a red dress to her shoulders and repeated, "It matches me!"

That's what any gift should do—match the receiver. It should please, satisfy a need or a wish or a secret dream. But matching gifts to grandchildren takes some doing. The value of a gift is not in its cost but in its suiting the child. Possibly the best gift is one that surprises by its unexpectedness.

Wise grandparents realize that gift-giving also fulfills a need in their own lives. We want to express love, and we want the grandchildren to love us. So we give. Make sure, then, as Paul Tournier advises in *Gifts,* that the ones we choose are not to satisfy our own pride instead of to please the child.

Affluent grandparents may indulge their own desire to be generous, considering at the same time their responsibility as stewards of their money. Those living on small fixed incomes, with little cash to spend on gifts, will find other ways to give.

Middle-income grandparents may budget the amount they spend on grandchildren, perhaps curtailing other gifts. As we grow older we tend to cut out "exchanging" with our contemporaries. Some shower and wedding gifts to mere acquaintances may also be eliminated.

Whatever the gift, it should be what we can afford in time, money, or possessions, wrapped in love.

When grandchildren are very young, practical gifts or toys may be best. We found with ours that what one child received at a certain age, the others also clamored for. We gave a succession of foam pillows, inexpensive luggage (for visiting grandparents and going to camp), sewing kits, jewelry boxes, electric alarm clocks, subscriptions to *Ranger Rick,* transistor radios, and finally watches.

A woman I know with many grandchildren gave each of them a desk dictionary when they graduated from high school.

One retired grandfather made doll furniture for his granddaughters when they were small. The actual cost of wood and materials was small. But he spent hours in his basement workshop sawing, gluing, nailing and varnishing the doll cribs, chairs, and cupboards, complete with drawers and shelves.

For birthdays and Christmas a grandmother who is

a superb knitter rotates giving beautiful sweaters, ponchos, and shawls to different grandchildren, remembering the others with lesser gifts.

Choosing the right gift for high school grandchildren takes thought and attention to their interests. Usually they prefer clothes or money. But clothes in the stores may be too expensive, and there's always the hurdle of correct sizes. Besides, many girls prefer to sew for themselves.

When I was puzzled about a confirmation gift, I said to a neighbor's boy, "You're the age of my grandson in the city. Do you have any suggestions for a gift for him? What would you like?"

"Ma'am," the boy said without hesitation, "send him money."

"Yeh, Grandma," someone else added, "Give him something that won't break, like a $20 bill."

Gifts of money, however, also take thought and tact. At one end are grandparents who can't afford frequent money gifts. Some wonder why a grandchild isn't excited about $1, or why a teen feels he's hardly struck it rich with $5. At the other extreme are grandparents who write $100 checks for birthdays, holidays, and other occasions, outshining all other donors.

Although grandchildren are seldom loth to accept a transfusion from the bank, parents may view such gifts as bribes. They may feel grandparents are trying to buy the children's love. This is especially true when the parents are hard-pressed for money and can't compete with the grandparents' gifts.

It's difficult for grandparents to understand this attitude. "Why shouldn't we be generous?" a woman I know said. "We have so much, and the kids are struggling to make ends meet. All we have will be theirs when we die. They need help now more than they will 30 years in the future. Why shouldn't we have the fun of giving the grandkids what their parents can't afford?"

Possibly the way the gift is given is what counts. One grandfather accumulated a bank account for his grandchildren. But he ran into trouble when he tried to give it to them.

"There's $4000 there now," he told his wife. "I'm going to give it to Tina when they come next week. She can buy whatever she wants for the kids."

"Here," he said, handing the bankbook to his daughter and her husband. "Buy the kids some nice clothes or bicycles or skiing equipment."

Neither the man nor his wife were prepared for their son-in-law's explosion. "Keep your money," he yelled. "We want to be independent."

"I thought you could use the money for things the kids need," the man said.

"No! They don't need anything. You keep giving them what Tina and I can't afford. I want to support my own family without handouts." Perhaps the son-in-law knew from past experience that his wife's father wanted praise, and he wasn't prepared to give it.

One son whose mother gave him substantial gifts of money told her, "I put it into investments to help with the college fund. I don't want to use the money for regular expenses." He too wanted independence.

The answer lies, I think, in directing unusual amounts to the parents, not the grandchildren, with no strings attached, or in building up a college bank account in the grandchild's name.

When grandparents give away their possessions, these too should be without restrictions. If a granddaughter uses the heirloom quilt for a table cover, don't blink an eye. If a grandson slaps yellow paint over the antique finish on the chest of drawers, keep still. If a grandchild sells the diamond as a down payment on a car, rejoice that diamonds have appreciated and he realized many times what the ring cost.

A man I know learned a lesson about giving with no strings attached. One of his expensive suits, in good condition, hung unused in the closet.

"Let's give this suit to Andy," the man told his wife. "The one he wears to church has holes in the seat of the pants."

A few weeks later the man grumbled. "Did you see my suit on Andy? He doesn't keep it pressed. Looks like he carries rocks in the pockets."

"When you gave it to him," his wife asked, "did you say anything about keeping it pressed?"

"Of course not." Then the man laughed—and gave up his suit.

Gifts for college students also take planning. "The best gift I received for graduation," says one girl, "was a thesaurus. Other gifts that came in handy were a box of notepaper with a stamp on every envelope. Also a pencil sharpener, an alarm clock, and a little plug-in pot for heating soup or coffee or cocoa."

Other thoughtful gifts might be folding money, a care package of brownies, instant coffee, cocoa, tea bags, and a letter, not expecting a reply.

Sometimes a grandchild wants a gift we would never think of. I remember the year Gary, in kindergarten, desired such a gift. To celebrate the country's Bicentennial his teacher asked if any child's grandparents had some object used in bygone days that they would be willing to bring to school for the children to see.

"My grandma will," Gary volunteered. Later he called me. "Grandma, you know your school bell? Will you bring it to my class and talk about the olden days?"

"Of course," I said. The bell, yes, but I wasn't so sure about the olden days. Still I had told my grandchildren that when I went to school the janitor rang a huge brass handbell (like the one I had) when it was time for classes to start. And that era might well be termed "the olden days."

I selected a few brass bells from my collection and went to school. Gary sat next to me and took charge of the bells. Afterwards the children rang them.

Giving to grandchildren takes love, time, and understanding. If their desires are beyond our resources or our ability to give, we can do what one salesman suggests, "Find out what people want and help them get it."

We can give cheerfully, not in competition with others, but what we can afford, making sure that the gift isn't merely to satisfy our pride.

Grandparents who are high-level givers have discovered, as Khalil Gibran writes, "It is when you give of yourself that you truly give."

That may well be the best gift—the gift that matches any grandchild.

Long-Distance Grandparents

For many grandparents in our society on wheels, knowing and understanding grandchildren—never easy goals—appear out of reach. The children may live half a continent away or even in a foreign country. Or, because of divorced parents, they may be somewhat inaccessible.

Many parents teach their children to keep in touch with grandparents. Others neglect to do so. But grandparents have an obligation, I believe, to make overtures of love and interest.

A father told me of a set of grandparents who neglected to make such advances. He and his wife had taught their children love and respect for his parents, who lived 2000 miles away.

"My parents are not well off," the man said, "so we never expected them to remember the children with big presents. A letter once in a while, or a birthday card would do. Children love to get mail. But my parents seldom wrote.

"When our daughter graduated from college and made a trip west, she wanted to visit her grandparents. They were too busy to meet her at the airport so she had to take a taxi both ways." No one would blame the young woman if she thought her grandparents weren't interested in her.

Long-distance grandparents who try to retain family ties and strive to understand their grandchildren will find their efforts pay off. Unselfish love that overlooks slights, neglect, and even criticism, love that never holds a grudge, that stretches across the miles and includes grandchildren, will work wonders.

The steps to keeping close to distant grandchildren include simple ones that most grandparents will readily think of. Be a learner. Stay alert to what's going on in the world. Write, phone, send packages. Visit them and invite them to visit in return.

Increased knowledge of world affairs and science makes it easy for children to outgrow their parents, let alone grandparents. Those who fail to stay abreast of the times widen the gap between them and wide-awake fifth- and sixth-graders. Teens will tune us out. We need to grow in knowledge with them and learn what it's like to be young today.

A national magazine recently carried a quiz on space age facts. After trying to answer the questions (all about kilometers, atoms, quasers, and the "Red Planet"), I admitted defeat. Plainly I needed a study course or two to keep me contemporary.

Better still, we grandparents can develop a lively curiosity that leads us to ask questions about what others are learning, especially our grandchildren.

A college professor told me, "It's impossible for anyone to keep up with knowledge in all fields. We should grow in our own areas of interest and learn to listen and ask questions in others."

Another step that ties distant families together is two-way mail. At first grandparents may send more mail than they receive. Although a grandbaby can't read, a letter will please parents and start a lifetime flow of letters, valentines, birthday and get-well cards.

"I remember the time my grandma wrote on my birthday card the meaning of my name," Natalie said. "When I wrote asking how she knew, she told me she had read a library book about names. Wasn't that neat she took time to look up my name?"

Some grandparents win honors writing little stories about pets and birds or even the weather. As the children grow we can write about good relations with other people and about how we put spiritual truths to work in our lives.

A young woman found that her grandmother helped her know distant cousins, aunts, and uncles. "When I was a child," she says, "my grandmother wrote me all about their achievements and travels. Last year when I flew to her city for a wedding and met some of those relatives for the first time, I felt I knew them."

One grandfather in his 80s, who excelled in letter-writing, mailed a birthday letter to each of his grand-children and later to his great-grandchildren. At last count he wrote to 38 a year, and he received plenty of return mail.

Phone calls too help us stay close to absent grand-children. We hear their voices and they hear ours. Long-distance phone calls can be budgeted just as treats are for on-location grandchildren.

Letters and phone calls show children (often with both parents working) that grandparents care.

If finances permit grandparents can send lavish birth-day and Christmas gifts. But gifts need not be expen-sive. It's the package the mailcarrier delivers addressed to the child that's important. Children appreciate a book, a game, a bracelet chosen with care. As they grow older, a gift from the grandparent's home will be treasured. A child will look at a small picture or figurine and remember Grandmother sent it.

Being on visiting terms is another way to shorten the distance between families. No matter how cordial the invitation, wise grandparents know their arrival will upset the family's routine, so they make the visit short.

Usually someone moves to the living room or rolls out a sleeping bag. Doug is very generous about giving up his bed when I visit. He even agrees to let me turn off the aquarium lights at night, and he's careful about choosing his clothes from closet and chest at times that don't disturb me.

As I packed to leave one time I said, "Tomorrow you can sleep in your own bed."

Cheerfully he replied, "That's one good thing about it." I thought his frankness was commendable. We understood each other. Both were glad to sleep in our own beds again.

Long-distance grandparents usually welcome an entire family for a visit, so there's little time to know any one grandchild. If possible, arrange for the grandchildren to visit one at a time for a few days. Even a preschooler knows attention is more concentrated when she visits alone. When she was only five, Pam printed a note, "Grandma, I want to come by myself this summer."

Most grandparents I've talked to advise plenty of rest before the clan arrives. One man says, "We stock up on food—snacks, candy, and milk. It would help if we had a cow."

Make the visit memorable with sightseeing and special events a child won't forget. Visit local historical or science museums. Take in a ball game, the children's theater, or the state fair. Once a grandchild and I climbed to the top of the spiral steps in the bell tower of a large church. We covered our ears at the loud bonging.

Older children love to browse in the shopping mall, and usually become lost. When they are trying on clothes no grandparent can locate them.

Living in the state capital as I do made it easy to learn state history along with grandchildren. We visited the capitol, heard a committee in action and the senate or house when in session. We climbed the circular stairway to an outside walk and admired the prancing gilded horses. Or we rode to the top of the highest building and scanned the horizon for miles. In the streets below, red and yellow bean-sized cars caught our attention.

It's important to give the same experiences and love to grandchildren whose parents are divorced, but it may be more difficult.

After her son's divorce, Stella rarely saw her little grandsons, who lived with their mother in another state. One Christmas Stella learned the boys and their mother would be visiting their other grandparents in a suburb 20 miles away. She called and asked if she might have the boys for a day.

"Why don't you come over here?" the boys' mother asked. "Save you all that driving. You can visit my folks too."

But Stella felt the time the boys would be in town was all too short, and she wanted to know them better.

"I don't mind the drive," she said. The total of 80 miles seemed little enough for the privilege of reading to the boys, playing games together, and having fun with them in her own home.

Another way for grandparents across the miles to draw grandchildren closer is to help them accept change. Frequent moves can be upsetting to young children and disruptive to teens. Leaving home, school, and friends, they feel the floor beneath them is giving way. Grandparents, having lived through many changes in their lives, can reassure the children that relocating is not a major catastrophe. It may even turn out to their advantage.

As we give of ourselves and our means without thinking of recognition or reward, as we learn about our grandchildren across the miles and are tolerant of their viewpoints, the young in turn learn about us.

For years the relationship may appear one-sided, with grandparents in a holding pattern, like a jet waiting for recognition. Then one day we hear the signal, "Cleared for approach." Touch down. And there's somebody waiting there we know.

Adventures
on Wheels
and at Home

"My son wants me to drive with them to California," a 60-year-old woman said. "I told him thanks, but no thanks." She added, "I don't care about seeing our country from the middle of the backseat with two kids climbing all over me. I'd rather stay home and look at their pictures when they return."

She is missing an adventure, a chance to grow closer to her grandchildren, to have an unforgettable trip, to be included in every picture.

Certainly such closeness will occasionally produce turbulence. Extensive togetherness will reveal it's next to impossible to match their liveliness. We may be content to lean back and watch the scenery. Children must be *doing*.

Still, a grandparent can, with good humor and imagination, devise ways to channel energy, resulting in adventuresome trips, vacations, or visits.

A station wagon holding three generations—dad, mom, five youngsters and a grandmother—can heat up like a pressure cooker. After a lengthy ride with squabbles escalating, one grandma suggested, "Let's make a set of rules for in the car. Bethy can write them down."

Ideas and complaints jumped up like popcorn. After some revision the children settled on these:

RULES FOR IN THE CAR

Don't fight in the car.

Sleep in the car or else you may spit up.

Don't take off your socks.

Cover your mouth when you are going to cough.

Be quiet.

Don't tap the driver.

Be polite.

Don't bother someone who is trying to sleep.

Try to be lovable.

The grown-ups agreed the rules covered problems reasonably well, and the children monitored one another.

On a long trip, when adults are beginning to feel unravelled and children are whining, a grab-box can produce smiles.

One out-of-town grandmother, learning her grandchildren and their parents were moving, stocked a carton with dolls, games, and surprises, and tucked in love notes. Then she mailed the box to her granddaughters to enjoy on the cross-country trip.

To make a grab-box, cut a narrow slot, large enough

to admit a child's hand, in the cover of a shoe box or another sturdy box. Fill the box with candies, a book of riddles, puzzles, crayons, scratch pads, a magnet and a few paper clips, miniature cars and toys, a game, a mouth organ. Add trinkets from the variety store or anything that will provide interest on the long ride. Be sure to include duplicates of candy or gum and enough prizes for everyone to draw several times.

After stuffing the box with prizes, seal it and decorate the outside. Add instructions that the grab-box be brought out once in the morning and once in the afternoon. Each child reaches in a hand, feels the objects with no peeking, and pulls out a prize.

Grandparents at times let themselves be trapped into promising a trip in the distant future. A friend says that in an unguarded moment she made such a promise. When her granddaughter teased her to take her to Europe, the woman said, "I'll take you when you learn a foreign language."

Some years later the girl reminded her of the promise. "Grandma, you said you'd take me to Europe when I learned a foreign language. Well, Grandma, I'm studying Russian."

A number of grandparents I know do take their grandchildren to Mexico, Europe, or Israel with happy results. Not everyone, though, can afford such trips. One sensible man, when his granddaughter begged to go to England with him, softened his no.

"Would you like to travel?" he asked the child.

"Oh, yes. I would love to travel."

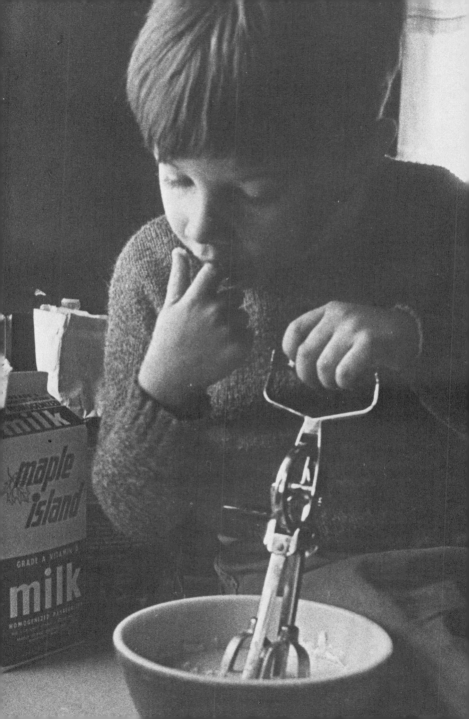

"I can't afford to take you to England, but how about a steamboat ride on the river?" For the time the child was satisfied.

A pastime for in the car as well as at home is memorizing scripture. Picture flashcards (prepared in advance by the children) will help them remember the words. Cut 4x5 inch cards from various colored construction paper. On one side print a Bible verse and reference. On the other side paste a picture which expresses the meaning of the verse. Search old magazines, Sunday school papers, calendars, and Christmas cards for suitable pictures.

The "I am" verses of Jesus—the door, the good shepherd, the vine—are easy to illustrate. So are Psalms 1 and 23, parts of 1 Corinthians 13, and others. When children learn the meaning of scripture through association with a picture, they understand it better than by repetition alone.

One family takes a carton of library books on trips. Reading aloud from *The Guinness Book of World Records* interests the whole family.

For adventures at home, grandparents might take a tip from Margaret Clarkson, teacher, poet, and writer, who suggests that adults should never buy anything children can help make. Even young ones can learn how to cook, sew, knit, hammer, paint, and refinish furniture. Such activities allow children to think—to prepare, design, or construct objects.

On stormy days or when a cold keeps them indoors, suggest that children write a story, a poem, or a prayer.

The story need not be long—just a few sentences telling how the child feels about something.

"First-graders can learn to write little stories," says a teacher. "I like them to write sentences with correct spelling. We talk about topics—a baby brother or sister, a pet, a storm, or a trip. Then they describe it on paper."

Feelings are important in writing poetry. "Children often are more imaginative than many adults," says a visiting poetry instructor for junior high classes in city schools. "They look at everyday objects in a lighthearted way."

Children might write a short prayer to read before the evening meal or at bedtime. Ask, "Who gives us our food? Our homes? Who watched over us today? Do you want to thank God for his love?" Help the child polish the prayer, then read it before meals a few times.

Or they might compose a letter by cutting the words from titles and advertising in magazines, then pasting them on a sheet of bright paper.

The granddaughter of one couple makes the Christmas greeting they send each year to friends and relatives. With crayons the child draws several Advent scenes and prints appropriate words below. Together they choose the best one and have it "zip printed."

One year the little girl drew a manger scene and printed above it the words, "Mare and Joseph and Jesus, I love you." The Js were backward, the letters crooked, but the child's imagination showed when she drew a heart for the letter *o* in the word love.

Another project that interests children is a depression garden. In an open dish put a few lumps of coal, porous brick, or even a sponge. Mix 2 tablespoons of salt, 2 tablespoons of water, and 2 of bluing. Pour over the coal and let stand 24 hours.

The next day add 2 more tablespoons salt. On the third day mix 2 tablespoons each of salt, water, and bluing. Add a drop or two of Mercurochrome or red vegetable coloring and pour over the garden. The chemical reaction will produce flowerlike growth. To keep the garden growing indefinitely, add more salt, water, and bluing from time to time.

It takes ingenuity to think of activities for trips, vacations, or home visits. But once their interest is sparked children will add their own ideas.

Talking to God

Two little girls visited their grandmother for a few days. At home before meals they prayed in unison, "Come, Lord Jesus, be our Guest. . . ." A beautiful prayer. But their grandmother chose her own words when she prayed.

At the dinner table one child said, "Grandma says so many different prayers."

· The older child replied, "She makes them up in her head."

"Oh, she couldn't." The youngest child was skeptical. She hadn't begun to talk to God herself.

Rather than repeating the same prayer over and over, which tends to become mechanical, children can learn a variety of written prayers. They can also express praise and thanks to God in their own words.

Grandparents can talk to God in plain words, not lofty sentences, avoiding, for the children's sake, the use of *thee* and *thou, wouldst* and *couldst.* Teach children to be specific, to pray for the neighbor with a broken leg or Aunt Martha in the hospital instead of everybody who is sick.

Grandparents should be careful not to preach at children in prayer. Rather let them hear our praise and thanksgiving for God's love and care and prayers for those in need and for the visiting grandchild.

Three-year-old Bonnie spent a few days with her grandmother while her parents vacationed. At the table she folded her hands as taught at home. Grandmother prayed, "Thank you, Father, that we can eat when we are hungry. Thank you that we can eat together and not be alone, for you have promised to be with us. Thank you that Bonnie could come to visit Grandma."

After a few meals Grandma left out the thanks for Bonnie's visit. Before she picked up her spoon the little girl said reproachfully, "Grandma, you forgot to say Bonnie lives here too."

The omission was quickly taken care of.

Besides spontaneous prayers in their own words, children can use what others have written to help direct their thoughts to thanksgiving.

Here is a table grace handed down in one family for several generations:

> For the hands that serve us,
> For the hearts that love us,
> For the grace that saves us,
> We thank You, O God, through Jesus Christ.

Another favorite, written by an unknown author, is:

Father, we thank you for the night
And for the pleasant morning light.
For rest and food and loving care
And all that makes the world so fair.

Help us do the things we should,
To be to others kind and good;
In all we do, in all we say,
To grow more loving every day.

Parts of various psalms make prayers children can understand and learn:

"May my words and my thoughts be acceptable to you, O Lord, my refuge and my redeemer" (Ps. 19:14 TEV).

"Open my eyes to see wonderful things in your Word" (Ps. 119:18 LB).

"Search me, O God, and know my heart!
Try me and know my thoughts!
And see if there be any wicked way in me,
And lead me in the way everlasting"
(Ps. 139:23, 24).

Older children can memorize Psalm 23 and the Lord's Prayer.

These two prayers from *Hello, God!* by Lois Walfrid Johnson will direct children's attention to God.

God,
You gave me ears
to hear the robins sing.
You gave me eyes
to see rainbows in the sky.

You gave me fingers
to feel my kitten's fur.
I like the way you made me.

It's great to stand on my head
and see things topsy-turvy.
You made things
so they look good
either upside down
or rightside up.

At bedtime children can recall the happy times of the day and praise God in their own words. Even a very young child can be taught the truth of Psalm 4:8: "I will lie down in peace and sleep, for though I am alone, O Lord, You will keep me safe" (LB).

Another of my favorites is by Carl F. Burke:

God be in my head and in my understanding;
God be in my eyes and in my looking;
God be in my mouth and in my speaking;
God be in my heart and in my thinking.

The essence of talking to God, I believe, is expressed by Herbert F. Brokering in "Let Us Pray."

Bow the head.
Fold in all thoughts.
Quiet the self.
Pray.

After That the Dark?

Our church was shocked and saddened when the two-year-old son of one family we knew took sick and suddenly died. A few weeks later at Bible study the young mother prayed, "Dear Jesus, thank you that our little son's soul is with you, that he will never be sick or hungry or lonely again." Although her heart was breaking, she believed the song writer's words, that her child was safe in the arms of Jesus.

For the other children in the family, it was their first encounter with death. "Why did God let Mikey die?" they asked. It's not an easy question to answer. Theologians and philosophers have struggled with the why of death since before the time of Job.

We have only to watch television or read the newspaper to see death and burial featured. But it's not something we are watching or reading about when death comes into our own lives.

Children may be bereft of a parent or grandparent. High school students may have to endure the sudden death of a classmate, killed by leukemia or accident. Psychologists tell us that it's the death of another, not the prospect of their own death, that affects very young children. It's the death of someone they love or depend on that worries them.

"Will Mommie die?"

"I hope you don't die, Grandma. Who will knit our mittens?"

"Why did God let Susie die? Who will I play with?"

Later, when children reach about nine years, they begin to understand that death is a part of life, that they too will one day die.

An 11-year-old girl told her mother, "I want to be with Jesus, but I'll never do anything to get there before he wants me."

"That's why Jesus sent his very own Spirit to live in us," her mother explained. "So we aren't lonely."

But death puzzles children and perplexes older teens and college youth as well. Many are grappling with the meaning of life after death. If Christ's message in all its fullness dwells in us, we will strive to help and comfort our grandchildren when the fear of death stalks them, especially if it's their own death that distresses them.

We need not be reluctant to say when difficult questions arise, "I don't know." We can explain that we are all refugees in this world, that heaven is the Christian's eternal home. "What man is he that liveth, and shall not see death?" (Ps. 89:48 KJV).

According to some psychologists, all of us should talk more about death and face up to our own. We can help grandchildren consider the truth that earthly life will end. When a pet dies, or when someone prominent in the news, a distant relative, or a neighbor dies, we can bring the talk around to the fact that all of us will one day die.

It's important, though, not to sugarcoat the facts with such statements as "Grandpa's on a long journey" or "Aunty's just having a long sleep." Never tell children anything they will have to unlearn later.

Johnny was only five when he began to ride his older brother's bike. Although he had been instructed about street traffic, he raced into the street without looking. His grandmother, who lived with the family, called him back sharply.

"Johnny, you can't ride the bike unless you are very careful," she said.

"Why?" He was breathless, red-faced, and perspiring. He hadn't time to stop and listen to a scolding.

"If you don't watch for cars," his grandmother said, "you may be run over and killed."

"What does 'killed' mean?"

"You would die."

"Well, if I die I would go to heaven and be with Jesus like my Sunday school teacher says."

"Sit on the steps," his grandmother said. "God has

given you your life and you must not be careless with it. God will decide when it's time for Johnny to go to heaven."

Then she added, "If you were killed and did go to heaven, it wouldn't be just for a visit. It would be forever."

A few days later a girl down the block ran into the street and was hit by a car.

"Gram," Johnny said, "Annie's in the hospital. She was careless with her life, wasn't she?" Johnny was beginning to learn about life and death.

A healthy attitude toward the value of life will carry over to teen years and adulthood. It will help young people understand that life is relatively short, that each of us is given only one body, and that it should be cared for.

A young mother with terminal cancer revealed what the shattering news meant to her. "Before," she said, "I was afraid of death and didn't like to think about it. Now that my doctor has told me I could die at any time, every moment of my life is precious to me." She paused. "And I'm ready to die."

Three jean-clad teens, who had just collided with the brevity of life, slipped into the pew next to me. When the service was over I talked to them.

The girl said, "We came to pray because a friend of ours has just been killed in a car accident." My heart went out to those young people as I offered my sympathy. It may have been their first encounter with death.

How can we help older grandchildren who face a

devastating death of parent, brother, sister, or close friend? In *Christianity Today* ("The Ones Who Are Left," Feb. 27, 1976), Elizabeth Eliot gives a practical suggestion for those who are deeply hurt by the death of a loved one: "Repeat the Creed." By focusing on the truths of the Apostles' Creed, grandchildren will consider the fact of death without dwelling too long on their loss.

A 92-year-old man had died, and his out-of-town children sat around the table after the memorial service comforting the widow.

"I didn't want any flowers except mine," she said. "But when an identical vase of red roses from you children and grandchildren came, I had to admit they were exactly right."

The daughter who had ordered the flowers by wire said, "I specified either yellow or red. Wasn't it nice the florist sent red?"

Another daughter said with a gleam in her eye, "I can just see Dad leaning over and instructing some angel, 'Be sure it matches the other vase of roses.' " Their father had been a take-charge man all his life, and the quip tickled the family. Recalling a trait of the man who had died turned their thoughts outward.

When a classmate of Greg's died in a traffic accident, his grandfather said, "Greg, I didn't know your friend very well. Tell me about him."

"Gramp, he was terrific. Best quarterback our team ever had." Then he spilled out a long account of their days at camp, their tryouts for the team, their plans to go to college together. In the telling Greg remembered his friend and forgot self.

A middle-aged man stood talking to the 30-year-old son of a neighbor who had just died. "Your father helped me find my first job," the older man said.

"He did? That was just like him. I guess my father helped a lot of boys find jobs." The reminder of his father's kindness brought comfort.

As we call to mind fine acts of the one who has died, we enable our grandchildren to consider the fact of death and the need to prepare for it.

While not fully understanding life after death, Christians have confidence in the goodness of God. Still we have questions. Death is indeed a mystery, and nearly everyone sooner or later is curious about the afterlife.

"Twilight and evening bell/And after that the dark!" I have never quite agreed with those words of Tennyson in his famous "Crossing the Bar." He may have meant "dark" as a symbol of the unknown, for in the end of the poem he says, "I hope to see My Pilot face to face." And seeing can't be done in the dark.

Life after death is, as Shakespeare's Hamlet asserts, an undiscovered country from which no traveler returns —no one but our Lord Jesus Christ. And because he lives we shall live also. Easter is a reminder of the promise of resurrection—new life after death.

Yet God has not left us entirely in the dark. The Bible tells us that we will know each other when we die and go to heaven, that we shall be active, without pain or physical handicaps, and that we shall be in the presence of our loving heavenly Father.

To cap it all, "Eye hath not seen, nor ear heard, neither have entered into the heart of man, the things which God hath prepared for them that love him" (1 Cor. 2:9 KJV).

All such thoughts can be expressed when our grandchildren confront us with questions about death.

Legacy

One evening as I watched television, world-renowned violinist Isaac Stern answered questions put to him by director André Previn.

"You can't teach young performers how to play," Stern said. "You only teach them how to listen." He picked up his violin and bow and played a few bars of a movement the way it was written. He paused for a moment, then played the passage again with his own eloquent interpretation. I felt fireworks off the top of my head and goose bumps up and down my arms.

A close look at our grandchildren and ourselves may reveal we can't teach them how to live their lives—only how to listen to others.

Can we interpret and transmit what we have learned from life's Composer so that our grandchildren will listen, so they will catch life's melody, its motif?

Self-centered children think about what they can get.

But already we are beginning to understand that the world doesn't hold enough resources to satisfy everybody's wants. It is the soul that needs to be satisfied. Believing that life is *now,* many young persons fail to see the present as a prelude to a lifetime.

By our interpretation of life, can they hear when they are out of tune or make glaring mistakes?

If our relationship has been built on love, admiration, and tolerance, they will listen. Without preaching we can try to put across the truth that responsible adulthood is not only a worthwhile achievement, it is a lifelong process.

It is even more crucial for grandparents to stand by when parents have failed their children through divorce, misdeeds, or blunders.

Not all grandparents have the resources to leave their grandchildren a cash legacy. Still, they possess intangible assets that overshadow real property.

Grandparents can provide solidarity by keeping up family traditions—birthday celebrations, oyster stew or lefse on Christmas Eve, picnic on the Fourth of July.

My husband's family holds an annual reunion picnic. All nearby aunts and uncles, cousins, in-laws, and new babies gather for the event. Mary Jo, one of the youngest, is working on the family history. For several years she has asked questions, listened to grandparents, written letters to faraway relatives. She has spent hours in city halls and museums, researching family birth dates, marriages, property ownership, and deaths. She has

compiled a vast amount of information, a valuable record for the Brandt family.

All-star grandparents will hand down the family's heritage, traditions, and oral tales. Preserving a family's pictures, records, letters, diaries, and possessions that have historical significance will help grandchildren catch a glimpse of their past. Those who lack such records often go to extremes to discover them. Adopted children frequently search for years for their real heritage.

In addition to helping children understand the importance of a family heritage, grandparents can encourage them to be curious about the present and set goals for the future.

When my parents married, my father's grandparents gave them a vase. A graceful reminder of the past, it is crazed with time. What interests me now is the letter that accompanied the gift.

Dear Beginners:

A few days ago we sent you a Bohemian vase. A vase is a good figure of what others can and can't do for you in your home life. It can simply hold the flowers you put in it. We cannot give the flowers. They must be picked by you—fresh every day. Our empty vase will be of little service to you unless you fill it.

Your loving grandparents

One day I shall pass on the vase and the letter to a granddaughter with the hope that her married life will be like a vase filled with fragrant flowers.

Our grandchildren may already be establishing their own traditions to hand on to their descendants, giving them a sense of family permanence.

A friend of mine showed me a wedding invitation she received from a niece. The young couple, who would be working in a home mission project, sent this note:

> We have everything we need. Instead of a wedding gift to us, please give to your favorite charity, or to the children's work where we will be going.

The young couple received more than $500 for the home mission. In addition, they established a family tradition.

Another asset we might pass on to grandchildren is the ability to face tough situations. "A laugh will calm down a shouting match quicker than angry words." I don't know who said that, but it's true, even when the going is rough. Finding something to laugh about oils the machinery.

There are times to roll up the sleeves, bend the back, pitch in, and change things. Other times there's nothing to do but wait or keep on going, like the title of a recent book—*I Can't Go On, I'll Go On.*

Records show that many conveniences we now take for granted were the product of years of difficulties and hard work. From idea to finished product ready for sale, antibiotics took about 30 years, instant coffee more than 20 years, television more than 60 years. Surely in all those years someone felt like running away, but instead kept on trying.

Possibly the most valuable asset we can pass on to our grandchildren is our love.

A woman said to me, "Aren't you assuming too much when you say young people are interested in all that old stuff? How about those two kids we read about in the paper last week—the ones who broke into homes and stole all that antique silver and jewelry and sold it for whatever they could get?"

Did someone fail those boys when they were younger? Did they have little acquaintance with love and family solidarity? Interest in family heritage needs to be fostered long before such escapades.

The motto on Joyce's wall read, "You'll find me under LOVERS in the yellow pages." Her friend Sandy stared at it. "Who gave you that?" she asked.

Joyce giggled. "My grandma. She gets these far-out ideas." Joyce paused. "But if I need help, she's right there."

Another bequest is the importance of faith in God. Most grandparents I've talked to declare life would be hopeless without faith in God. They agree with the grandfather who says, "I want my grandchildren to stand beneath the cover of Jesus Christ's righteousness. I don't want them to be Bible-peepers only. I want them to discover God's will for their lives."

That's a big order. And as Henrietta Mears, authority on teaching young people, once noted, "It's easier to teach the facts of Genesis than to help a youth discover why he is here and what Christ's will is for him." The habit of talking about the providence of God and answers to prayer will highlight our own faith.

Still another asset we can transmit is a forgiving spirit. Others have told me one of the greatest agonies they have experienced is seeing their grandchildren enmeshed in sin—shoplifting, drugs and alcohol, pregnancy outside marriage.

A woman I talked to said, "We had such high hopes for Meta. Now—" Then she added, "The sickening part is our wounded pride and embarrassment."

There's no need to feel anger and rejection. What's needed is compassion and forgiveness.

In the Gospels Jesus tells the story of a father who welcomed back his prodigal son. Nothing is said about grandparents, but if the father forgave without asking questions, how much more should grandparents?

A minister speaking on forgiveness said, "No one could ever displease or wound us more than we have displeased and wounded the Father in heaven. No one."

Yet God through Jesus Christ has forgiven us. And this leads to the biblical principle that we should forgive one another—in shattering experiences and in day-by-day brushes with family and friends. We need to forget the past, focus on the present, and work toward bright days ahead.

More valuable than money in the bank, securities, jewelry, or real estate, are the intangible assets we leave our grandchildren when the song is over.